MW00816505

Come, Christians, Join to Play!

Creative Hymn Settings for Piano Four-hands

Mark Hayes

Editor: Larry Shackley
Cover Design: Jeff Richards
Music Engraving: Lyndell Leatherman

ISBN: 978-0-7877-1419-2

A Lorenz Company • www.lorenz.com

Foreword

Playing piano is one of the joys of my life, and if you are reading this, I suspect it is for you, too. The only thing better than playing a solo is sharing the joy with a partner on the bench. I have received many positive responses to my first four-hand piano duet book, *Great Things He Has Done.* Inevitably I'm asked the question, "When is the next piano duet book coming out?" You now have it in your hands, this time with even more selections than the first book.

Three of these arrangements are special because of their dedications. I wrote the "ragtime-esque" rendition of "Since Jesus Came Into My Heart" for Sarah and Eileen Huston. Sarah is Eileen's granddaughter and they have spent a lifetime making music together. "Joyful, Joyful We Adore Thee" was written as a gift for the parents of Marta Neill and Natalie Oppel, who are sisters and love playing together. Brian Lee and William Phemister are known as the Chicago Piano Duo. Dr. Phemister is Professor of Piano Emeritus at Wheaton College and Dr. Lee is Professor of Piano at Moody Bible Institute. The setting of "O the Deep, Deep Love of Jesus" I wrote for them is certainly a difficult arrangement, but it's worth the challenge. For a piece with fewer notes and a gentle feeling of repose, you may enjoy "My Shepherd Will Supply My Need". There truly is something for everyone in this book.

Mark Hayes

Contents

Come, Christians, Join to Sing

Mark Hayes
Tune: MADRID
by **Christian H. Bateman** (1813-1889)

Duration: 3:10

4

6

10

To our parents, Ralph and Joyce Neill, with immeasurable love, respect, and deep gratitude for their gift of music and in celebration of 50 joyous years of marriage.
Marta and Natalie

Joyful, Joyful, We Adore Thee

Mark Hayes
Tune: HYMN TO JOY
by **Ludwig Van Beethoven** (1770-1827)

Duration: 3:00

LL

My Shepherd Will Supply My Need

Mark Hayes
Tune: RESIGNATION
from *Southern Harmony,* 1835

Duration: 2:35

LL

Dedicated to Eileen and Sarah Huston to honor their years of making beautiful music
together as grandmother and granddaughter; piano teacher/accompanist and student

Since Jesus Came Into My Heart

Mark Hayes
Tune: **McDANIEL**
by **Charles H. Gabriel** (1856-1932)

Duration: 2:40

70/1945L-31

Battle Hymn of the Republic

Mark Hayes
Tune: BATTLE HYMN
19th c. American Folk Song

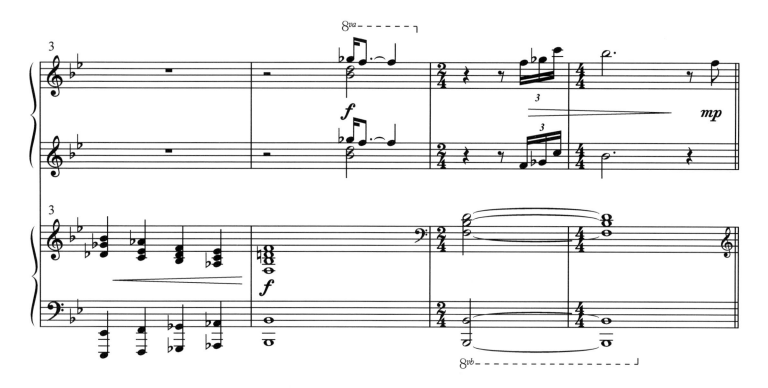

Duration: 4:00

LL

40

70/1945L-40

Ding-Dong! Merrily on High/
O Sanctissima

Mark Hayes
Based on Traditional Carols

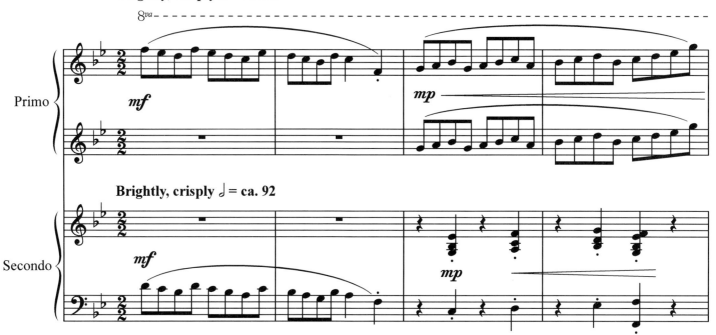

Duration: 2:55

Ding-Dong! Merrily on High*

Branle l'Official from *Orchesographie*
  by **Thoinot Arbeau** (1589)

70 **O Sanctissima***

*Tune: **O Sanctissima**

Tattersall's *Psalmody* (1794)

for William Phemister and Brian Lee, The Chicago Piano Duo

Oh, the Deep, Deep Love of Jesus

Mark Hayes
Tune: **EBENEZER**
by **Thomas J. Williams** (1869-1944)

Duration: 4:10

LL

58

70/1945L-58

60